American Girl Library

W9-AZY-499

MORE HELP!

By Nancy Holyoke
Illustrated by Scott Nash

PLEASANT COMPANY

Published by Pleasant Company Publications
© Copyright 1996 by Pleasant Company

First Edition.
Printed in the United States of America.
96 97 98 99 00 KRH 10 9 8 7 6 5 4 3 2 1

American Girl Library® is a trademark of Pleasant Company.

Editorial Development by Peggy Ross and Roberta Johnson
Art Direction by Kym Abrams and Jane S. Varda

Library of Congress Cataloging-in-Publication Data

Holyoke, Nancy.
More help! : another absolutely indispensable guide to life for girls! / by Nancy Holyoke ;
illustrated by Scott Nash. — 1st ed.
p. cm. — (American Girl Library)
Summary: Presents more letters written to "American Girl" magazine
by girls asking for advice about the problems they face in everyday life.

ISBN 1-56247-481-2
1. Girls—United States—Life skills guides. 2. Girls—United States—Conduct of life.
3. Interpersonal relations in children—United States.
[1. Conduct of life. 2. Letters.] I. Nash, Scott, 1953– ill.
II. Help! III. Title. IV. Series: American Girl Library (Middleton, Wisconsin)
HQ777.H66 1996 070.4'44—dc20 96-11550 CIP AC

Dear Reader,

American Girl magazine gets more than 300 letters a week from girls all over the country asking for advice. A year ago, we collected some of these letters into a book called *Help!* Readers liked it so much we decided to do it again. And so . . . here's *More Help!*

Each girl you'll meet here sat down to write with a troubled heart. The letters are full of feelings—hurt and anger, doubt and sadness. Feelings all girls share.

Will you find advice you can use? We hope so. We also hope you'll remember these girls the next time you see someone at your own school who needs a helping hand—and give her yours.

Your friends at *American Girl*

Aargh!

Dear *Help!*,

I have trouble doing things that my mom tells me to do, like:

    (1) shower

    (2) make my bed

    (3) be nice to my sister

    (4) get straight A's.

Aargh! I need help!!!

Crazed in California

When you walk, you put one foot in front of the other. Each step takes you about a foot. Twelve inches may not seem like much, but a girl can get anywhere that way. Remember this when Mom's expectations seem out of reach and you're feeling crazed and hopeless. Pick ONE problem—say, organizing your time in the mornings. Shut out all the rest. Think the problem through and come up with a couple things you can do that might help. Make them your assignment for the week. You'll make a little progress and feel a little better. In other words, if you can't do it all, do what you can. You'll be amazed how far a girl can get chugging along step by step. By step.

Adopted

I am adopted. I told my friend Sally, and she told the biggest gossip in the school. Now everyone knows, and they are asking me questions. What should I do?

a different girl

Kids who don't know anything about adoption are often curious about it, and that's why they ask questions. If you don't want to answer, don't. Just say, "I don't want to answer that. It's too personal." On the other hand, there's no reason to hide the fact that you're adopted. So tell your parents what's going on. They can help you find the words to express your feelings about adoption in a way that makes you comfortable. The big surprise may be just how good this makes you feel.

Bad Influence

My friend and I have been best friends for three years. My mom and dad love her. The problem is that they also think she does improper things, which I will admit sometimes is true. They say she's a bad influence and want me to stop being friends with her.

Wanna Stay Friends

Your parents are afraid you'll start talking, acting, and thinking like your friend. So don't do it. Hold on to your own good judgment and don't *let* her influence you. And when your parents don't like the way your friend acts, tell her so. Say, "My parents don't allow swearing" or "My dad thought you were rude yesterday." Speak up yourself for what you believe is right. Be a good influence. If your friend can change her ways, maybe your parents will change their minds.

Best Friends

Dear *Help!*,

A long time ago I was best friends with my next-door neighbor, Katie. Now I have a new best friend. I still want to be friends with Katie, but not best friends. How can I tell her without hurting her?

Helpless in North Carolina

Well, the truth is, you've already hurt Katie. Her feelings were hurt as soon as you began spending more time with your new friend than you did with her. If you make an announcement like "You're not my best friend anymore," she's going to feel worthless. So give Katie the same kindness and attention you give the other girls you count as friends. If she asks why you are spending so much time with this new girl, say, "I like her a lot, but that doesn't mean you and I can't still be friends." Which is true.

We can still be friends.

Dear *Help!*,

I have a friend named Laura. She is good in art and is teacher's pet in almost everything. She is very nice and has many friends. When she plays with one of her other friends and not me, I get jealous and mad. I like Laura so much, and I want to be her best friend. But how can I when she has so many other friends?

Jealous

When you're crazy about a friend, it's natural to want that friend to be crazy about you. But you can't tell a friend how to feel. Laura *wants* to play with other girls. Getting jealous and angry won't change that. It will only make Laura think you're trying to hog her. So whenever you're with Laura, relax and enjoy yourself all you can. Chances are, she'll enjoy herself, too. Will that make you her best friend? Not necessarily. But it will make Laura happy to see your face when she sees it next.

Blabbermouth

Dear *Help!*,

I'm bad at keeping secrets. Every time someone tells me a secret, I blurt it out. I'm afraid my friends won't like me if I keep telling their secrets.

Ally

You're right. Your friends *won't* like you if you blab. So how do you stop?

Plan 1: The next time you're tempted to open your mouth to tell a friend's secret, imagine her face when she hears what you've done. If that doesn't help, go to . . .

Plan 2: When a friend says, "I'll tell you something if you promise to keep it a secret," plug your ears. Say, "Don't tell me, please! I can't keep my mouth shut. I'd rather keep your friendship than try to keep your secret."

Blushing

Dear *Help!*,

Whenever I get embarrassed my face gets real hot. When it happens in school, someone always says, "Hey! Your face is *so* red!" That makes me even redder.

Embarrassed

When you're embarrassed, your nerves send extra blood into the tiny blood vessels in your skin. Doctors call this *vasodilation* (VA-zo-di-LA-shun). The rest of us call it a blush. Blushing is a reflex— you do it without thinking—and that's why it's so hard to control. Keep in mind that all kids let their emotions show. Some do it by tears, some by temper. You blush. It's *natural*. As you get older, you won't be embarrassed as easily and will probably blush less. For now, when you feel a blush spreading, think of something cold, like ice water. That might help. And if a kid hoots, "Hey! Your face is *so* red!" just shrug and say, "I can't help it. I'm one of those kids who vasodilate a lot."

Bossy

Dear *Help!*,

Whenever I'm in school or somewhere else where we have to work in groups, everybody says that I'm bossy. I think it's because when I have an idea that I think would help, I want them to be quiet so I can tell them. That really doesn't help, so what do I do?

R.S.

For starters, don't talk too much. After you express an idea, wait till at least three other people have had their say before you open your mouth again. Do this even if you don't agree with what they say. Second, when the others are talking, listen. *Really* listen. Don't sit there rehearsing what you're going to say next. Finally, when you speak up again, be sure that what you say shows you've heard what the others said. Remember that sometimes the biggest difference between a bully and a leader is being able to l-i-s-t-e-n.

CAR WASH

Boys

A boy in my class is my friend. We aren't boyfriend and girlfriend. We are just friends. Sometimes people make fun of us. It's really bugging me.

Erica

It's perfectly fine for girls and boys to be pals. Kids who don't understand that miss out on some wonderful friendships. Luckily, you're too smart to let that happen to you. Tell yourself this teasing is plain old peer pressure. Your best bet is to take the least popular but most effective advice of all—ignore it.

Boys

Dear *Help!*,

My friend and I like the same boy. I don't want to mess up our friendship, but I want the boy to like me, too. Is there any way I can get to know him without hurting my friend?

Baffled in Buffalo

There's no getting around the fact that you and your friend want the same thing, but it makes no sense to argue about who "gets" this boy. It's up to *him* to decide if he likes one of *you*. So tell your friend what you've said here: "I like Bob, too, but I don't want to mess up our friendship." Suggest to her that you get to know him together, and make a pact to put friendship first. If you want to talk to Bob during recess, invite your friend to come along. If you want to sit with Bob at lunch, save a spot for her as well. Most of all, don't do anything to hurt this boy's opinion of your friend. If you're kind and honest, you may find three can have a lot of fun.

Dear *Help!*,

Do you have any advice for when you like a boy and find yourself acting very weird around him?

Lost

Saying "relax and be yourself" is sort of like telling you to jump over the moon. It's the right answer, but 99 percent of girls find it impossible to do. So if you can't relax, do the next best thing. Don't try to impress him. Don't talk big—or smart or tough or sweety-sweet. It's better to seem a little goofy than to seem like a phony.

Bras

Dear *Help!*,

I'm going into fifth grade. All my friends wear bras. I asked my mom for one, but she said I didn't need one. I feel left out. Please don't tell me it doesn't matter. It does to me.

Left out

Start by telling your mom how you feel, and ask if you can spend your own money to buy a bra. If the answer's no, you might try layering your shirts and other tops. That way, no one can tell whether you're wearing a bra or not. You may still feel left out, and that's no fun, but you may also feel less self-conscious, and that could help.

Brothers & Sisters

Dear *Help!,*

I have a little brother who's six. I love him, but I'm constantly hearing "Don't fight with your brother" or "Be nice to your brother." I love my parents, but I have a terrible feeling in the pit of my stomach that they love him more.

Sick to My Stomach

Many, many big sisters have days when they feel as you do, but, truly, your parents don't love your brother more. Look at the families around you. Don't you see pretty much the same thing?

Most parents expect older kids to be understanding of their little brothers and sisters—to compromise, to share, to let them have their way. This has everything to do with how old you are and nothing at all to do with how much they love you. If it still doesn't feel that way, pick a quiet moment and ask your mom or dad for a hug. With their arms around you, your heart will know the truth.

Brothers & Sisters

Dear *Help!*,

My sister and I fight a lot. I'm not quite sure why, but when we don't fight I like to play with her, and I realize how much I love her. I want to stop fighting with her, but how?

Wanting to Stop

Sometimes fighting becomes a kind of habit. You do it without thinking, especially when you're bored. To stop the fights, make yourself aware of what you're doing. Tie a string on your finger or put a sticker on your hand. When bickering begins, the string will remind you that you don't want to fight. Grab on to your temper, and go find something fun and interesting to do instead. Finally, make a resolution to surprise your sister by doing one nice thing for her every week—something that will make her sit up, blink, and exclaim, "Gee, thanks!"

Dear *Help!*,

My sister is turning into a total teenager. I feel like we're growing apart. Please help me. She has started to talk on the phone endlessly and get interested in boys. Please don't tell me that this is all about growing up. I just need something to say to her.

Lonesome

Picking the right time to talk to her may be more important than some secret formula for what to say. Don't try to pull her away from her friends. Instead, look for quiet moments of the day when you're alone with your sister—say, when you're getting ready for bed or setting the table. Ask about her friends. Ask about the boys. Ask about anything you know she likes to talk about. Then listen. You may not care a whit about that stuff yourself, but it's a way to show you care about her. Truth is, this *is* all about growing up—but that's good news, not bad. It's good because it means your sister won't be like this forever. She'll continue to change, and so will you.

Brothers & Sisters

Dear *Help!,*

I have three younger sisters, and they are *triplets!* They are all two years old, and believe me they are not angels. I've got babysitting overload. I've tried talking to my parents and having a friend come and help me. What am I going to do about this impossible problem? I have no social life.

It sounds as if your parents are as over-loaded as you are—and in no mood to let you relax with a friend in your room while your sisters run them ragged on the other side of the door. Try this: Ask if you can sign up for some organized activities once or twice a week. If your parents think you're doing something worthwhile, they may be more willing to let you go. You might also ask if you can divide your time differently. If you babysit every Tuesday and Thursday afternoon, maybe you can have Wednesdays and Fridays off to go to a friend's.

Camp

This summer, my mom is going to make me go to a summer camp. I would much rather just stay at home and play with my friends and go to the beach with my family. I don't see why she wants to waste her money. But she says, "You'll have lots of fun." What can I do?

Reluctant Camper

A lot of parents don't want their kids "hanging around" all summer with little to do. Is that your mom's worry? If so, you could propose a schedule of activities that would keep you active and learning if you stayed at home. If she still wants you to go, decide you'll make the best of it. See if you can find a friend to go with you. Read about the camp. Choose your favorite activities. Then pack up your clothes and your sense of adventure, and have a smile ready for the girls you'll meet on the bus. By the end of the summer, they'll be your good friends.

Class Clown

Dear *Help!*,

I have great friends, but I always feel I have to prove myself to them by being funny. At the end of the year, I got an award for being most likely to become a comedian. I don't want to be remembered as class clown.

TOO goofy

There's not a thing wrong with being funny or having a reputation as a comedian. All the same, you're smart to know you shouldn't hide behind the laughs. Great friends, like yours, love you for who you are—not because you entertain them. So start thinking of yourself as class scientist or class writer or whatever else you'd rather be. When you set off for school tomorrow, put a rubber ball in your pocket. When you feel yourself getting goofy, give it a squeeze. Pretend the ball is a clown's nose and tell yourself, "I'm not wearing this today."

Clothes

I love to dress up in fancy, wild, and casual clothes. I love putting together outfits. But whenever I put an outfit together, this girl in my class criticizes it, and I feel totally stupid. This girl acts like she's the queen of romance and fashion, even though we're only in the fourth grade.

Fashion Conscious

No way should you let this girl bully you into dressing her way! If you want to wear striped leggings with your polka-dot dress, do it; if you want to wear earrings made of Froot Loops, do that. Decide for yourself what you like. This doesn't mean you'll always come home happy with the outfit you wore. It does mean that learning to dress is about finding your *own* style—not learning to conform. You can tell that to the Queen of Fashion, too.

Competing

Dear *Help!*,

I'm on a soccer team. When we lost a couple of games, a few of the girls started saying, "Oh, we're going to lose the rest of the games," and I don't think that's true. How can I get them to think positive?

Wanting to Win

(1) Talk to the coach.

She may not realize how bad these other girls feel. So tell her. She may have all sorts of ideas that would help.

(2) Compliment your teammates.

Losing can be frustrating, and too often players criticize each other as a result. Do the reverse. Everyone has different strengths. A few words from you about a good play or a special talent could give a girl the confidence she lacks.

(3) Be a good example.

Keep your mind on the game. Don't think about the score or your mistakes or what your mom's doing on the sidelines. Play as hard in the last few minutes when you're five points behind as you did at the half when the game was tied. And play to win. You'll make good things happen for your team—and you could be the spark that makes other girls catch fire and play hard, too.

(4) Look for the small victories. When your friends are moaning about a loss, remind them of something good or funny that happened during the game—say, the moment little Mimi stole the ball from the big forward with the green shoes. It will help break the gloom and remind these girls that any game is a lot more than the final score.

Copycat

I have a friend who copies everything I do—my hair, my clothes, etc. It bothers me a lot. I painted my room light purple. A few months later, she wants her room painted again. She painted it the same EXACT shade of purple. Everyone should have her own style. Why copy me?

Mad in Massachusetts

Because she has no confidence in her own taste—and a lot of confidence in yours. She admires you! What you need to do is tell her nicely that you don't like being copied, but you'd be glad to give her advice when she's getting her hair cut or picking out clothes or anything else. Then—and this is important—when she makes a choice, compliment her. Let her know you respect her choices. Then maybe she can begin to respect them herself.

Crybaby

Dear *Help!*,

I'm too sensitive. I cry over every-thing. Then people make fun of me. I try not to cry, but I can't help it!

Crybaby

It sounds as if you've got more feelings inside than you can hold. See what happens if you put some of them into a journal. Write every day. Write about things that have happened to you. Write about people you know. As you express yourself on paper, you'll be untangling thoughts and thinking to yourself about problems you face. This may help you

express your feelings to other people in words. The more you can say in words, the less you may need to say in tears.

Disabled

Dear *Help!*,

I am handicapped and just moved to a new school. Suddenly, I am getting special treatment from other kids. I HATE THAT. I wish they'd stop treating me like I'm broken.

Elsie

These kids may be going about it the wrong way, but the fact is, they're trying to be nice. So talk to your teacher. She can introduce the subject of disabilities in class. Once your classmates get the basic facts, they'll be more able to treat you naturally. You should also practice speaking up for yourself. There isn't a thing wrong with telling a kid in a friendly way, "Thanks very much, but I can do this myself."

Divorce

My parents fight a lot. It always makes me scared that they're going to get a divorce. Mom will say, "No, honey, we're fine." But then I listen through the door to the basement or the laundry chute. What should I do?

Upset

When parents fight, it can be *so* hard and *so* scary. Yet some arguments can help solve a problem. Others go away when a situation changes. Your mom might be right—the marriage could be fine. For now, you might feel better if you stopped eavesdropping on these fights. Make yourself listen to the radio instead. If you can't help but overhear your parents' angry words, let them know how this made you feel. It's O.K. to ask for reassurance. It's O.K. to ask if they're going to a counselor to resolve their differences, too. Just remember that if there's a problem with the marriage, only your mom and dad can fix it. No one can do it for them—not even you.

Divorce

Dear *Help!,*

My parents are divorced. My dad lives in New Mexico. He is always promising that he will call me, write me, or come and visit, but he never does, and that hurts me.

Hurt

Write him a letter and say so, as plainly as you can. Does your dad realize how many promises he's broken? List them. Does he think his visits and phone calls don't matter to you? Tell him they matter a lot. Why does he keep talking about tomorrow? Say you need to know he loves you today. It might do you good just to write this sort of letter, and it might well do your father good to receive it.

Dear *Help!*,

My parents are getting a divorce. I only see my dad on Saturday, and I do not think this is fair. It's hard to do this with my dad. My sisters and I are sad when he leaves for a week. How can I deal with this change?

A Girl Who Misses Her Dad

This *is* hard—terribly. Talk to both your parents about how you feel and say you'd like to have more time with your dad. Can you and your sisters spend one night a week at your dad's, or at least have dinner with him? Or can you stay with him on Sundays every other week? These are questions you have a perfect right to ask. On days you can't see your dad, call him and fill him in on what happened that day—and do the same with your mom when you're staying at your dad's.

Divorce

My mother and father got divorced about five years ago. I live with my mom. I would like to get married and have kids some day, but I'm afraid that I might get divorced and I wouldn't want my kids to go through what I had to. I know it's a long way off, but I think about it.

Worried

P.S. I talked to my mother about it, but she didn't know what to say.

A girl can inherit a lot of things from her parents—the color of her skin, the shape of her nose. But a divorce? No. No way. There's just no reason that your future has to be like your parents' past. Make up your mind to take what you've learned from your parents' mistakes and use it to avoid mistakes of your own. For now, pack up the question "Should I get married?" and store it in a corner of your brain. When the time comes to take it out, you'll know the answer.

Fame

Dear *Help!*,

I am ten years old. I live in Tennessee. I know what I want to be: an actress and a supermodel. I am really determined to be those things, but when you live in an unfamous state like Tennessee it's hard to be recognized for your talent and become a big star.

Beth

Your average Famous Person started out life as a regular kid—a kid who was good at some things and not so good at others, living an unfamous life in an unfamous place. A kid, in other words, exactly like you. So don't worry a bit about being from Tennessee. What will matter to you are things like brains, talent, determination, looks, luck, and plain hard work. Just stick this thought in your pocket: Happiness doesn't come from seeing your face on the newsstands. Happiness comes from loving what you do and liking who you are.

Fear

Dear *Help!*,

I'm afraid of getting kidnapped. Sometimes I go too far, like when people are nice to me in the village shops, I think they're trying to kidnap me. I have bad dreams about being kidnapped at least twice a week. I talk to people about it, and that helps a little.

Scared in Kansas

(1) Keep talking.

It *does* help, you're right. Scary thoughts and dreams lose power when you think about them out loud with someone you trust. An adult can also remind you

that, despite awful stories you may see in the news, abductions by strangers are very, VERY rare.

(2) Don't bite off more than you can chew. If going to the village alone scares you, don't do it. Instead, ask your parents to help you master your fear bit by bit. Go to town with them. Let them introduce you to clerks they know. Locate the public phones. Talk about what you should do if you ever feel threatened. Where should you go? To whom should you turn? Get to know all the public places you might visit. When you feel ready, practice going into the stores alone while your mom or dad is nearby. After that, do some errands with a friend. Chip away at the fear little by little, and give your confidence a chance to grow.

(3) Remember, you're NOT powerless. Follow the three W's: Never go anyplace with anyone unless your mom or dad knows WHERE you are, WHOM you're with, and WHEN you'll be back. Keep in mind that if you find yourself in a situation that makes you nervous, you have every right to tell an adult how you feel and ask for help. Finally, tell yourself that you have a lot of control over your own safety. Because you do.

Freckles

Dear *Help!,*

I don't think I'm pretty. I have a ton of freckles all over my face.

Not Pretty in New York

When you look in the mirror, all you see are your freckles. Yet chances are, your friends hardly see them at all. They look at you and see—well, *you.* They see the brightness in your eyes, the curve of your smile, the expression on your face—your whole personality shining through your features. That's where beauty lies, not in how close you come to looking like a model. Try to believe that. And this, too: Almost everyone likes freckles except the girls who have them.

Friendless

I have no friends at school. Sometimes girls will be my friend, then use me and leave me. Everyone around me has friends. I feel so lonely sometimes I cry. I'm really a nice person but no one likes me. I can't figure out why. I feel so worthless.

All Alone

Look around you one more time. Do you see anyone else who's alone a lot? How about the quiet girl from the next class who stands by herself on the playground? Try offering some friendly words to her.

Sign up for some after-school activities, too. A girl who ignores you now might see you differently if she learns you're as interested in tree frogs as she is. Finally, look for friends outside of school. Take a class in ballet, karate, art, or whatever else sounds fun. The more active you are, the happier you'll be— and the better chance you'll have of meeting a girl who's smart enough to see what a terrific friend you'd make.

Frustrating Friends

Dear Help!,

I have a friend who doesn't like to clean up. Whenever we play with things, she goes home and leaves the cleaning to me. When I tell her we have to clean up, she says, "Let's leave it out and play with it tomorrow." Or she stuffs it in the closet, like, "I'll hold it while you shut the door." I've tried confronting her, but she says, "That's the way I am."

The Maid

If you and your friend plan to play a game that involves a lot of stuff, go to her house. When the two of you are playing at your house, keep it simple. Set out a small number of games or toys ahead of time and keep the rest off-limits. If your friend wants to pull things off the shelves or out of the closet, say, "No. I don't want to clean it up by myself." If she wants to play with it, she's got to promise to put it back.

Dear *Help!*,

Whenever my friend comes over to my house, she always has to get what she wants or she goes home. I try to do the same thing at her house, but all she says is "Fine. Go home."

Jennifer

Your friend is bullying you, and if you really want her to stop, you'll have to call her bluff the way she calls yours. The next time she threatens to walk out, keep your cool and say nicely, "Maybe it *would* be best if you left. Maybe we shouldn't play together today." Then go to the closet and hand this gal her coat. The message will be very clear. You aren't going to let her win an argument with threats.

Gangs

I'm in fourth grade. I have to go to a certain junior high school when I'm in seventh. My sister and I are scared to go there. My sister has to go there next year and, boy, is she scared. Why? Because there are gangs! We've heard of these gangs! We're so scared!

Scared Stiff

Rumors can be scarier than facts. So for starters, work with your parents and sister to find out what's really going on in this school. Talk to the principal, the teachers, the police, other parents. Talk to kids who go there. Are gangs really a menace? If so, what's the community doing to solve this terrible problem, and how can you and your family help? Also, what advice do these people have for kids like you? Should you stay away from certain places or avoid wearing certain clothes? The more you know, the safer you'll be, whatever the situation. Most of all, be sure to choose the right friends—friends who want to keep as far away from gangs as you do.

Gossip

Some of my friends are talking behind my back. Whenever I'm around them, they act as sweet and innocent as a cupcake. It bothers me to think they would do that.

Truly Bothered

You're right to be bothered. If your friends have a bone to pick with you, they should come to you and say so. *Psst-psst*-ing about it with other kids is simply two-faced. Your best bet is to talk to these girls honestly. Try not to accuse them. Instead, *tell* and *ask*. Tell them what you heard. Tell them how it made you feel. Ask them straight out, "Did you really say those things about me?" Perhaps you can talk it out and clear the air. And if you can't? If your friends still aren't honest with you? Then you can't trust them—and it's time to start looking for friends you can.

Grades

Dear *Help!*,

My mom expects A's and some B's in my school grades. But on my last report card my math grade went from an A+ to a B–. I told her things were just getting harder. But she won't let go. My math teacher said, "Don't push her," but Mom won't listen. I feel she expects too much.

frustrated in Colorado

You, your mom, and your teacher should have a conference. Discuss how and what you should study each day, and the amount of time it should take. If the three of you can come up with a study plan that addresses your mother's concerns, maybe she will agree not to push you about your grades. Then it's up to you to follow the plan. If you truly try your best, you can be proud of yourself no matter what grade you get—and your mom should be proud of you, too.

Gross

On my bus, there's this really gross kid who says things that are so sick it's embarrassing to tell anyone, even my mother. I'll go to the front of the bus, but he'll follow me. Then he'll say he's sorry, but two seconds later he'll do it again.

DING!DING!DING!DING! The alarm's going off—and it's *loud*. Please, please tell your parents about this kid. Ask them to come with you to talk to the principal. What's happening here doesn't sound like a goofy gross-out ("The worms crawl in, the worms crawl out . . ." and stuff like that). It sounds more like an assault. The school should know about it, his parents should know, the bus driver should know. This boy's got to hear it loud and clear from all sides: Either he leaves you alone or he walks.

Haircut

Dear *Help!*,

I have a short haircut. A lot of kids at my school ask me the same question: "Are you a boy or a girl?" In front of all my friends! It really embarrasses me, but I hate long hair and I hate dresses.

a girl

Don't think for a minute that these kids have really mistaken you for a boy. They're teasing you, plain and simple. The best answer to "Are you a boy or a girl?" is "If you don't know the difference, you better talk to your mom."

Home-schooled

Dear *Help!*,

I'm in fifth grade, and I just started home-schooling. Everywhere I go, people have conversations about school. I feel embarrassed because they don't understand about home-schooling. They say, "That's weird" or "Don't you miss your friends?" What should I say?

Elisabeth

People will take their cue from you. If you look at your shoes and mumble, "My mom makes me do it," they'll think you've got something to be embarrassed about.

Look them in the eye instead. Explain how home-schooling works. Explain what you like about it and what you don't. For example: "I like getting my studying done more quickly and having more free time. I do miss my friends, but I still get to see them in the afternoons." There are hundreds of thousands of kids home-schooled in America today—so, you see, it's really *not* weird at all.

Homework

Dear *Help!*,

I'm not very organized. Sometimes I don't do my homework, and I'm in deep water with the alligators. Please help me find a way to be more organized and help me to remember to do my homework!

Unorganized

Here's a recipe for getting your work done using some very basic ingredients:

1 spiral notebook
1 calendar
1 alarm clock
a dash of self-reliance

Step 1. The notebook:
Label a spiral notebook "Homework." Take it to school every day. When you get an assignment, record it here. Draw an alligator on the cover to remind you what will happen if you forget.

Step 2. The desk:
Take a look at your desk or work area. Do you see loose papers? Scrunchies? A peach pit? Off they go. There should be nothing on it but a calendar and your schoolbooks. Period.

Step 3. The time:

Set a certain time for doing your homework, and do it at that time every day. If you find yourself cheating, set an alarm clock when you come in from school. When it goes off, you go to your desk and sit down. (It doesn't hurt to ask Mom or Dad to encourage and remind you, too.)

Step 4. The planning:

So you're at your desk. Before you do anything else, read over your assignments and write the deadlines on your calendar. Which ones are due tomorrow? Which ones are due after that? If you have a big project, break it into smaller pieces: "Go to the library." "Read about snails." "Write report." "Do graphs." Write each step on a day of your calendar, too.

Step 5. The doing:

First do the assignments that are due tomorrow. Then check your calendar and decide what you should do next. You're the boss. Now follow your own orders.

"I Hate My Name"

Dear *Help!*,

My name is Rosemary. I hate my name. All my friends have cool names. All the people I read about have good names, too. I feel like I'm the only one in the world without a good name. I want to change it, but my parents won't let me.

Rosemary

Is there a nickname you like? Rose or Rosie or Ro? If so, ask your friends and teacher to call you that. Remember, too, that names go in and out of fashion every bit as much as clothes. In 1900, the name Mildred was hot. In 1925, Betty was in the top ten. In 1970, Michelle seemed to be everywhere. Ashley came along in the 1980s. The point is this: "Rosemary" may seem geeky to you today, but it could be the coolest name on the planet tomorrow. So tell yourself you're a trendsetter. You have your own style, your own brain—your own name.

Klutz

Dear *Help!*,

I'm a klutz. Every time I turn around I break something, whether it's a bone in my body or my mom's best vase. What can I do?

Queen of clumsiness

It's a good bet that you aren't clumsy because you're a klutz. You're clumsy because you're growing. When a girl's in a growth spurt, her hands and feet get bigger before her arms and legs do. Till her arms and legs catch up, she has less control of those big hands and feet. So what should you do? Keep active in sports.

Slow down by the china cabinet. Be patient. You're going to grow out of this.

Left Out

Dear *Help!*,

I have two good friends. One, in front of my face, will say to the other, "Do you want to spend the night?" The other will say, "O.K." I don't have the courage to say that I feel sad and left out. Please give me some advice.

Feeling left out

Ugh! This is so rude! Your friends should have better sense than to do this—better sense and kinder hearts. If you can't find the courage to express your feelings directly, try this: The next time you ask one of these girls to do something special, do it by phone. Say, "I didn't ask you at school because I didn't want to hurt Mary's feelings. I really hate it when someone does that to me." If she doesn't take the hint, she doesn't care about your feelings. Start looking around for friends who will.

Lies

One of my best friends is always making up stories about things at school, and what she can and can't do. She is a very nice person, and I like playing with her, but I never know when she is telling the truth.

fed up

It sounds as if your friend doesn't think much of herself and thinks she has to lie to be liked. She's making a big mistake. Her lies will cost her friends, not make them. So tell her how you feel. Say, "You're a great person, but when you say you can speak German, and I know you can't, it really bothers me. It makes me wonder about everything you say. I don't care if you speak German, but I do care if you're dishonest." She may get angry. She may also think twice before she tells a lie again.

Locker Room

Dear *Help!*,

This year, I'm in seventh grade, and we have to change into gym clothes every day for Phys Ed. I'm not very thin, and we change in the locker room in front of other girls. I really don't feel comfortable about doing this! That may sound dumb because we're all girls, but that's how I feel.

Uncomfortably Shy

It doesn't sound dumb at all! Changing in a locker room is very different from changing at home. The best thing is to get it over with as quickly as you can.

Don't slow yourself down looking for girls who might be looking at you. Pay attention to what *you're* doing instead. Tell yourself that half the girls are worried about getting to their next class on time, and the other half feel just like you.

Mooch

Dear *Help!*,

When my best friend and I go to a candy store, she asks me to buy her something. I do. But she never pays me back.

always buying

A lot of girls find it hard to say no, but that's precisely the word you need here. This girl is taking advantage of you. The next time she says, "I would gladly pay you Tuesday for a Tootsie Roll today," say, "No. I'm not going to lend you any money until you pay me the $2.60 you owe me." She may give you some grief; don't give her a cent. Maybe the next time you go shopping, she'll remember to bring her purse.

Not until you pay me the $2.60 you owe me!

Movies

Dear *Help!*,

My mom is very strict about what movies I see. All the movies that she lets me see are too babyish for me. I'm ten, and she barely lets me see some movies rated PG!

W.D.

Your mom has her own ideas about what's right for a girl your age. There's nothing you can do to change that—which is why you're feeling so frustrated. What you *can* do is change your mom's opinion of how mature you are, in the way you fulfill responsibilities and handle disagreements just like this one. Will acting mature this afternoon get your mom to let you go to the movie tonight? No. But it could make her stop and think, "Wow, my daughter's really growing up."

Munching

Dear *Help!*,

I'm ten, and I'm a little overweight. I tend to watch TV a little more than I should, and the TV room is right next to the kitchen. When I watch TV I tend to eat things like chocolate chips and potato chips. I mean, I have an after-school snack, but it seems when I munch I never get full.

A Little Chubby

You're a smart girl to realize that your munching is part of your TV habit. Now, here's what to do. When you come in from school, get yourself a snack—one good snack that fills you up. Then tell yourself, "No more food till dinner." If you watch TV, give yourself something to do with your hands besides eat. Play solitaire or write in your diary or tickle the cat. Better yet, don't watch TV at all. Ride your bike or kick a soccer ball or walk the dog. Instead of gaining weight, you'll be taking it off—and you may have a lot more fun to boot.

New Glasses

Dear *Help!*,

I just got reading glasses, and I hate them! Everyone in my class thinks they're cute. How can I grow to like them?

Frustrated

Glasses feel odd when you first wear them. Everything seems brighter. Even the pencil on your desk suddenly seems to stand out. And, of course, when you look at yourself in a mirror, the glasses seem to stand out, too. You may feel like a Martian—and think you look like one, too. Truly, this is often a matter of giving your eyes time to adjust. Your friends say your glasses are cute. For now, why not believe them?

Old Car

Dear *Help!*,

This may sound funny, but, well, you see, my family has had an old Cadillac for ten years and I love it very much. But my dad said since it doesn't run anymore, he's going to take it to a place where they are going to smash it up, so we can get some money for it. I don't want my dad to do that!

a Sad friend of a car

Good times rub off on the objects people touch and care for every day. A car becomes more than a car. It's the family trip you took last summer. It's the day your sister spilled Coke on her head in the backseat. Still, what's the better future for the car you've loved so well? **(a)** It sits in your driveway, rusting until parts fall off. Or **(b)** it gets recycled, and its steel may be used again in a new car, which another little girl can spill Coke in. Really, the answer's pretty clear. So take a picture of your old car, then say goodbye. Let the tow truck have the metal. You have the memories.

Only Child

Dear *Help!*,

I'm an only child. As fun as everyone thinks it is, sometimes it's lonely. I've asked my mom and dad if they would ever have another baby, but they never answer.

Lonely

If you've told your parents how much you'd like a brother or sister, you've done about all a girl can do to get one. Now the decision is up to them. Don't sit around waiting. Check out the rest of your family—your larger family. Do you have cousins near your own age? Get to know them better. If your cousins live far away, ask your parents if you can invite them for a visit in the summer. How about second cousins? Aunts and uncles? Make a friend of everyone in the family you especially like. You'll feel less like the only kid in a family of three and more like one of the clan.

Partners

Dear *Help!*,

In school we have partners. My partner makes me do all the work, and she just copies what I write.

Doing All the Work

If this girl is just lazy, tell her straight out how you feel. If she's copying because she's struggling with the material, take a deep breath, try to be patient, and give her some help. In either case, talk to your teacher. Partnerships are rarely equal, and she knows that. But she should have ideas for how to make this one more fair.

Peer Pressure

Dear *Help!*,

Most of my friends hang out in one big group. Somehow they end up talking about someone—she's ugly or she's nasty, etc. I don't like this. If I try to talk to my friends about it, they get real angry at me!

Mixed up

Have you seen Kristen today?

Can you believe what she's wearing?

Totally gross!!

People do all sorts of things when they're in a group that they wouldn't do alone. It's as if they think there's one way to be—to look, to talk, to think. If a girl's different—*boom!* The group is saying mean things and sometimes doing mean things, too. You're right not to like it, and doubly right to speak up. If you can find the courage to hold your own opinions, maybe the other girls will wake up to what they're doing and feel ashamed. As they should.

Pentecostal

Dear *Help!*,

I belong to a Pentecostal church. I can't wear pants, cut my hair, or wear jewelry or makeup. A lot of people tease me. They call me Ms. Conservative and Long-Haired Smart Aleck—and I'm not a smart aleck.

Picked on

Too many kids spend too much time on the Science of Cool—how to dress cool, act cool, be cool. It makes them blind. They can't see a nice human being standing three feet away if she's wearing the "wrong" look. What do you do with kids like this? You can try explaining nicely that the way you dress is part of your religion. It's possible that some kids don't understand this, and would stop teasing you if they did. You can also go with your parents to talk to your teacher, who may have her own ways of getting these kids to lay off. In any case, stick with the kids who care about what you're like *inside* and respect you for standing up for your beliefs.

Pets

Dear *Help!*,

I love my dog. I can't remember a time when he hasn't been there. He's twelve. So am I. He has a hard time breathing, and his hearing is nearly gone. His eyesight is bad, too. My mom and brother are thinking of having him put to sleep. They say he is in a lot of pain. I would have no problem putting him to sleep if he could tell me that's what he wants. I can't stand the thought of losing him! Please help!

Hopeful

No one can tell you whether you should put your dog to sleep. Hard as it is, you have to make up your own mind about that. But talk to your vet. Does she think your dog's in pain? If so, is there anything that can be done to help? How long does your vet think your dog will live? Ask all the questions you can. Use the answers and the love you feel for your dog to help you make a choice.

Dear *Help!*,

I have a hamster named Yo. When I bought him, he was nice, but now he's really mean. I brought him to school for a class, and he bit two people, including my teacher. Now everyone calls him Lucifer!

Stumped

Put yourself in Yo's shoes. Or cage, rather. A trip to school can be a scary thing for a pet. Imagine being in a strange classroom. The world is a wall of new faces. Loud voices boom. Big fingers waggle at you through the bars. An enormous hand appears and grabs for you . . . ***EEEEK!*** No girl should keep a pet that bites, but if Yo has calmed down since you brought him home, he probably just can't take crowds. So give him what he needs: a quiet room and a second chance.

Piano Lessons

Dear *Help!*,

I hate piano lessons! They are so hard! They make me so mad! I stay on the same page for such a long time. My younger sister is very good at it and progresses quickly.

Unhappy

If you sit down to play hating the piano, your anger will build with each wrong note till you can't see the music in front of your face. So wipe your sister out of your mind. Tell yourself it's O.K. to go at your own rate. Then ask your teacher if you can learn a piece that you especially like. Practice this and only this till you can play it easily and well. Play it loud. Play it soft. Use the pedals. Sing along. Have fun with it. Then go back to your regular book. The next time your head's about to pop off with frustration, play a couple bars of your special piece. The music will soothe your temper, restore your confidence, and remind you that there's joy to be had if you stick with it.

Picky Parent

Dear *Help!*,

Let me get straight to the point. My mom is too picky. I'll get my room sparkling clean and dust our furniture almost perfect, but she seems to always find something wrong. Sometimes I spend my whole weekend doing chores. Help!

Tired

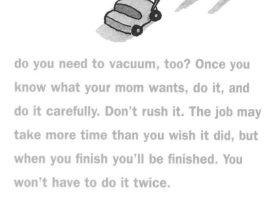

When you have a chore to do, talk to your mom *before* you start about how she wants it done. Can you dust around the clock, or should you lift it up and dust beneath it? Can you sweep the floor or do you need to vacuum, too? Once you know what your mom wants, do it, and do it carefully. Don't rush it. The job may take more time than you wish it did, but when you finish you'll be finished. You won't have to do it twice.

Pink

Dear *Help!*,

My room is almost all pink. I don't care for pink anymore. When we moved in I was six, and I loved pink. I got pink curtains, carpet, desk, and bed. I want to get new colors, but my parents say no. When I walk in I feel so weird. It's just too little for me now.

Sick of pink

Adding other colors to your room will cut the pink and give the room a jazzier, older feel. Try dark colors, like dark purples and blues, even black. Scrounge around the house. Put a blanket or an old table-cloth at the foot of your bed. Spend your own money to get some small pillows for the bed and a throw rug for the carpet. Cover the desktop with a blotter or a big sheet of paper. Sew or pin buttons onto the curtains like polka dots. Finally, ask yourself if there are other things in the room that make it look too young. If so, store them away.

Popularity

Dear *Help!*,

When I'm at school, very unpopular people come and ask me to play with them. I don't want to because I'm afraid I'll get unpopular.

Confused in Fort Worth

Being unpopular isn't like the flu—you don't catch it from someone who's got it. Still, it's certainly possible that the snobs in your class will make fun of you if you play with someone they think you should ignore. So here's your choice: (a) You can ignore the kids the snobs ignore and be a snob, too. Or (b) you can play with the kids you want to play with. If you choose (a) you'll be safe from the snobs. If you choose (b) you'll be free of them, and on your way to leading your own life.

Race

Dear *Help!*,

I just moved to a new town. I am black. In my old town, there were plenty of black people, but here there are hardly any. People look at me weird. Some kids tease me. I even think that some parents don't want to let their kids play with me and my little sisters. How am I ever going to make friends?

different

Being the new girl on the block is never easy. If people are prejudiced against your race, it can be one of the loneliest and most painful things in the world. But there *are* things you can do:

(1) Take another look at your neighbors, and talk—*really* talk—to your mom and dad. Do they see as much prejudice in this town as you do? Do *they* think you can make friends here? If so, where do they think you should start? Can they help you break the ice? Let your mom and dad know how you feel, and ask for their help.

(2) You might also try to hook up with other black kids in your area. There must

be some place African-American kids get together—a church, say, or a community organization. It will feel good to talk to other girls who know what it's like to be black in a white town—to share experiences and to exchange advice and tips of all sorts. Having black friends might make you feel less alone in this new place, even if you don't see them every day.

(3) Get involved in organized activities, both in and outside of school. Get out on the soccer field. Get a seat in the orchestra. Join the science club. The girls you meet will share your interests, and when you're sitting side by side trying to hit C-sharp, race will matter a whole lot less.

(4) Put your favorite photo of yourself on your bureau. *That's who you are.* Whenever you get one of those "weird" looks, tell yourself that. Remember the heroes who've fought in this country's battle with racism, and let confidence shine in your eyes. Sooner or later friends will come along who see and admire that.

Race

Dear *Help!*,

I have some black friends and like them equally as my white. My dad hurts my feelings because he uses a terrible word when he talks about blacks. I don't want to grow up being prejudiced! I feel very uncomfortable. Please help!

NOT Prejudiced

The next time your dad uses a racist word, tell him you don't like it. Say, "Please don't use that word. It's racist." If he keeps it up, or gets mad, leave the room. You can't stop your dad from talking this way if he's determined to do it, but you can let him know that he doesn't speak for you. You don't believe that people who are different from you are worth less than you. Say it firmly. Say it often. Let it guide your life.

Roller Coaster

Dear *Help!*,

When my family goes on a roller coaster, I get nervous. I'm scared of high heights and going upside down. I don't know how to cure it!

one scared-stiff girl

There's nothing odd about being scared on a roller coaster. You're supposed to be scared. That's the whole point! Some people like that scary feeling. You don't. That's perfectly O.K. A girl who goes on carnival rides isn't braver or better than a girl who doesn't. If you dread getting on a ride, don't make yourself do it.

Second Choice

I know two girls. They're in my class and they're always together. I like them, but they treat me like the odd-ball, the second choice. When one's out, I'm the one the other turns to in class. But it makes me feel bad, to be the second choice.

Second Choice

Hanging around a pair like this can make a girl miserable. They're just too wrapped up in each other to care about how you feel. Yet it seems they're your first choice of friends—and that's what has to change. Don't wait around for them to notice you. Make up your mind to get to know some other girls better. You'll feel a lot less left out if you're busy laughing and talking and working with someone else.

Sharing a Room

Dear *Help!*,

I have to share a room with my sister. She bothers me a lot. When I want to sleep at night, she keeps talking to me. If she's gone and I try to get some privacy, she comes barging in on me. I've tried talking to my mom, but the only other room that isn't occupied is the garage.

Going Nuts

You can't sleep in the Chevy, so better try a Sisters' Constitution instead. Ask your mom to sit down with you and your sister to write up a list of promises the two of you agree to make to each other about the room. For example: "I won't talk after lights-out." Or "I always have the right to enter my own room, but if the door's closed I'll knock first." Then both of you should sign the paper and hang it on your bedroom wall. This idea won't give you a room of your own, but it might well give you a better roommate.

Sleepovers

Dear *Help!*,

Whenever I go to a slumber party everyone disagrees. Some girls want to stay awake and some want to sleep. Then lots of people cry.

Sleepy and mad

The solution is to have one room for girls who want to sleep and another for girls who don't. Girls can lay out their sleeping bags in the snooze room when they first arrive. As the night goes on, sleepy girls can go to bed one by one, and party girls can party without stepping on someone's head.

Eight Tips for a Super Sleepover

1. Don't invite too many girls. The party will get wild, and your friends are more likely to break up into cliques. Five guests max.

2. Have at least three big activities planned for the night. Don't try to wing it by thinking up activities as you go. Trouble starts when guests get bored.

3. Check your supplies. If you plan to make cookies, buy the chocolate chips the day before.

4. Discuss the rules for the party with your parents before the party begins. Set a time for lights-out, and announce it to your friends soon after they arrive.

5. Be sure to have extra board games and a deck of cards sitting around the party room. They'll give you something to turn to if any of those big activities you planned don't work out.

6. No rough stuff. A pillow fight may sound like fun. In real life, girls get shaken up and things get broken.

7. Beware of truth-or-dare. A game that encourages girls to tell secrets leads to embarrassment and humiliation. Skip it.

8. And, of course, let sleeping girls sleep.

Smart

Dear *Help!*,

I'm smart, with a straight-A average, and friendly to almost everyone. Just one problem: Everyone thinks I'm a goody-goody. Some kids think it's not cool to be smart, but I know they have to be wrong. Right?

Right. In every school, there's a group of kids who spend their time cutting down achievers and trying to convince people that nothing's cooler than being bored. Hooey. The truth is, it's a ton of fun to use your brain at school. Good grades lead a million places you want to go. Boredom leads nowhere. So if you're not showing off—and it doesn't sound like you are—then you've got every reason to be proud. You're on the right road. Stick with it.

Smelly

Dear *Help!*,

One of my really good friends smells like a fish. I don't know how to tell her. What should I do?

Amy

Telling a friend she smells can be tricky. The problem comes up most often with girls who don't realize they have to bathe more frequently as they get older. In your friend's case, the smell may have something to do with what her family eats. It could have something to do with cultural traditions as well. If the smell is strong enough that you and other kids notice it and dislike it, she ought to know that. So who should tell her? Try talking to your teacher or the school nurse. They probably have more experience with situations like this, and can find a kind and private way to offer this girl a tip.

Sports

Dear *Help!*,

I'm twelve and I love sports. My town does not let girls play many sports. For instance, the boys play regular baseball, but the girls play softball, which uses a bigger and softer ball. The boys get uniforms, and all the girls get are T-shirts. I know many other girls feel the same way, but I don't know what to do.

Sports Lover

Write a letter to the head of the base-ball program pointing out how girls are being treated differently from boys and suggesting—politely—that this isn't right. Ask all the other girls to sign your letter. Make lots of photocopies. Mail the original to the head of the program, and a photocopy to every other adult who has a say in it, including all the coaches. (Ask your parents to review the letter and help you gather names and addresses.) Your letter's sure to get people talking, and that's the first step toward change.

Dear _Help!_,

I'm no good at sports, and I hate them. But my best friend likes to play sports, and so do all the other kids in my class. At recess, I just sit out and watch. My teacher told me to just join in. I did, but I'm not good, so people yelled at me.

Bad at Sports

Do something else! Swing on the swings. Jump rope. Play jacks or hopscotch or four square. Play Chinese jump rope or cat's cradle. Read a book or write a poem. Chat with other kids who aren't in the game. Do anything but sit and watch. If you still feel left out, ask your friends and family to work with you on basic sports skills a little every day. Practice throwing and catching balls. Practice kicking and dribbling them. Play the games they play at school. After a month, rejoin the games at recess. You'll still make mistakes—everyone does, including the kids who yelled at you. But the ball will feel more natural in your hands, you'll do better, and you'll enjoy it more.

Stepfamilies

Dear *Help!*,

My parents are divorced and Mom's getting married again. Her boyfriend's acting like my real father, telling me what to do, and what I can and can't have. What should I do?

Lauren

It's hard to have someone act like a dad when you don't feel like a daughter. So talk to your mom. Tell her that you know you'll have to obey her boyfriend eventually, but ask if you can have some extra time to get to know him better before you do. Ask for their patience.

Then make it a point to do some fun things with your future stepdad. Go to a movie together. Throw a baseball in the yard. As he becomes more a part of your life, it will seem more natural for him to enforce the rules. And don't worry that you're betraying your father by getting to know your stepfather. Your dad is still your dad. Nothing is going to change that.

Dear *Help!*,

My father just remarried. I have
two stepbrothers, one older and one
younger than me. I try to think of
them as brothers, but as much as
I try to love them, it seems like we
fight all the time.

Trying in California

It sounds as if you were an only child
before your dad remarried. That means
you're learning to be a sister and a step-
sister at the same time. That's a big,
big change! Plus, your brothers may be
struggling with how they feel about the
new family and taking it out on you. So
confide in your dad, mom, and stepmom,
and ask for advice on getting along with
the boys. But be patient. If you don't
love these guys yet, that's O.K. Love
can't be delivered in a moving van like
a new sofa. Love grows. *You're trying
to love.* That's the absolute best thing
in the world you can do.

Teased

I'm not very pretty and not at all popular. I don't have very many friends. Last year some kids teased me and even stole some of my stuff. The torment was every day, and I'm not exaggerating. My mom says they did it because they were jealous, but I have nothing that they could be jealous of. Please help.

Desperate for Respect in Oklahoma

The adults who run your school are responsible for making it a safe and decent place for every child, including you. When teasing gets this vicious, it's time for them to step in and call a halt. Ask your mom or dad to go with you to talk to your teacher and the principal. Is this tattling? No. It's more like calling the police. If these kids have stolen things from you and torment you daily, you deserve protection and they deserve to be exposed. You sound like a nice girl. This mean crew would be wise to envy you that.

Teddy Bear

Dear *Help!*,

I am in the seventh grade and I still sleep with a teddy bear. I really like sleeping with him. I feel kind of safe. My teddy bear is like a best friend to me. I've slept with him since I was three. It's a habit I wish I could stop. It prevents me from sleeping over at friends', and having them sleep over with me.

help needed

If you don't make a big deal about your bear, your friends won't, either. When you go somewhere to spend the night, stick your teddy bear in the bottom of your bag. When it's time to go to sleep, pull him out. If your friend says, "You still sleep with a *bear*?" say, "Sometimes. He's cute." Let it go at that. You can say the same thing when a friend sleeps over with you. Who knows? Your friend may sigh with relief, dig into her bag, and grab a fuzzy friend of her own.

Too Busy

Dear *Help!*,

When I get home from school, I have so many things to do! (1) I have to do my homework. (There is usually a *ton* of it.) (2) Practice the piano. (3) Practice the violin. (4) Study for a test (usually). I don't have time to do anything fun! I don't want to quit anything.

A Girl in Solon, Ohio

Make up an after-school schedule. Set aside a time to study, a time to practice, *and* a time to have fun. Be very official about this. Write down, "**5-6 p.m. Have FUN!**" And when the clock strikes five (or whatever time you pick), take a break from your studies and your music and goof off. A little free time will make you feel a lot less busy, and you'll go at your tasks—**1, 2, 3, 4**—with a fresh brain and good spirits.

Too Tall

Dear *Help!*,

Some people say I'm smart, funny, and nice. All people say I'm tall. Boys say, "So how's the weather up there? Ha ha."

too Tall for words

Girls start growing faster than boys at about age ten. By twelve, girls tend to be taller. A girl with tall parents may be a lot taller—and feel like a stork in a flock of ducks. But take heart. This is not going to last forever. By the time you're out of middle school, the boys will have picked up the pace, and many will be

your height or even taller. In the meantime, stand up straight, look these boys in the eye, and say, "The weather's just fine, thanks."

Trying to Be Brave

Dear *Help!*,

I have a sickness called epilepsy. I was diagnosed a few days ago. I guess you could say I'm a little ashamed about it. I know I shouldn't be, but I am. I've got so much on my mind! My parents think I'm being brave about it, but I'm not. Sometimes when I'm alone in my room I just break down and cry.

Ashamed

Of course you cry! Any girl would! It's scary to be told you have to live with a disease, and lonely in a terrible way. But being brave doesn't mean locking up your feelings. Let your parents know you're sad and scared. Ask them to hold you! It's also important to learn about epilepsy. Write down every question you have, including things like "Should I tell my friends?" and "What if I get sick at school?" Show the list to your parents and your doctor and get some answers. You'll soon begin to see epilepsy for what it is—a medical condition. *There is nothing shameful about it.* Two million Americans have epilepsy, and most lead very normal lives. Tell yourself that you will, too.

Trying to Be Nice

Dear *Help!*,

I have this girl in my class. She shows off a lot and she cries a lot. A lot of people tease her. I have a lot of friends. I don't want her to be my friend, I just want to help her be a regular girl. How can I help her?

Rita

By showing your friends and classmates how to forgive this girl for her mistakes. Don't make a big deal out of it when she shows off. Don't roll your eyes or make a face if she cries. Don't gossip about her. Most of all, when you hear other kids talk about her as if she had no feelings, remind them that she does. When you see them teasing her, speak up and say it's mean. If you can make even a handful of kids more tolerant, this girl may be able to relax and feel more like a regular girl—and more able to act like one, too.

Uninvited Guest

Dear *Help!*,

I have a good friend who always calls and invites herself over, even if I don't want her to. What should I do?

Erin

Option 1: **The next time this girl calls and says, "Can I come over?" say, "No. This isn't a good day." Don't get drawn into talking about reasons she can't come. Keep saying no politely and firmly till she accepts it.**

Option 2: **Ask your mom to help. It may be easier for her to tell this girl what she needs to hear: "We like having you**

here, but let us invite you. Please don't invite yourself."

Unloved

I have a problem. Here it is: I feel like my family doesn't love me anymore. I'm always getting into trouble, getting yelled at or sent to my room. I can't stop being naughty. I don't want this unloved feeling anymore.

Unloved

Your parents are angry and frustrated, and when you look at them you see it in their eyes. The miserable feeling this gives you may be one reason you're finding it hard to stop being naughty. So write your mom and dad a letter that says you're really lonely and miss feeling close to them. Ask each one to spend some time with you in the next week, just to talk and have fun. Also, ask yourself if something's going wrong at school or with your friends. Sometimes bad feelings can leak from one part of your life into another. If you can fix the other problem, you may find it easier to stay out of trouble at home, too. If none of these ideas work, talk to the counselor at school. Helping kids is her job. Give her a chance to help you.

Worrywart

Dear *Help!*,

I am worrying about the stupidest things lately. I'm turning into a worrywart! The worst thing of all is that I'm turning into the kind of people who write in to you with all those problems. I really don't want to turn into one of those people. What should I do?

Not wanna be like them

When worry is steaming up the windows of your brain, throw them open. Talk to people—your parents, your sister, your brother, your good friend, anyone you like and trust. What do they think? What would they do? Asking for advice doesn't mean you're a wimp. It doesn't mean you can't solve your own problems. It means you're resourceful. You can learn a lot from other people. Best of all, when worries are brought into the open air, many of them dry up and blow away.

the real YOU

Dear *Help!*,

My friend tells me that more people will like me if I look for the real person I am inside me. I don't know who that real person inside me really is, but I want people to like me. What should I do? I like the way I am now!

Worried in Vermont

If your behavior is causing you problems with other kids, work to change it. But don't twist yourself up like a pretzel looking for some mysterious other "you." Instead, pay attention to your feelings. Be honest, with yourself and with others.

Listen to other people but think for yourself. Never do something to make people like you if it's going to end up making you like yourself less. Now check out the mirror. Is there any doubt whose face is staring back?

Zilch

Dear *Help!,*

I'm going into middle school. Last year I was the best—a queen, everything. Next year, I'll be nothing, nada, zippo, zilch. HELP!

Rebecca

Well, you've got a point. Older kids tend to set the styles and call the tune in any school. But get out a photograph of yourself from kindergarten. Think—*really* think—about how far you've come since then. How many times have you been new and green and felt you couldn't do it? And how many times did you find that you could? You're a capable girl! Besides, you're not going to middle school alone. A lot of your classmates are going, too. You can figure it all out together—talking, playing, laughing, learning as you always have. Being top dog at your old school gave you a lot of confidence. Make up your mind you're going to take that confidence with you.

Even More Help!

A big problem can make you feel as if you're looking at the world from the bottom of a hole. You feel cut off from other people—even from those who love you best. Help seems a million miles away.

It's not. You don't have to face your problems alone. If you haven't found the advice you need in this book, look to the people you trust. Talk to your parents, grandparents, neighbors, friends. Talk to teachers and counselors at school.

These people can't solve a problem for you, but they can help in a big way. They can listen to you when your heart is sad. They can suggest solutions when you think you've tried them all. They can hook you up with people in the community whose job it is to help kids like you.

Gather up all the advice and ideas you can find. Try one thing, then another—and keep at it till you find something that works.